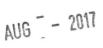

NERO: RUTHLESS ROMAN EMPEROR

Gareth Stevens
PUBLISHING

Please visit our website, www.garethstevens.com. For a free color catalog of all
our high-quality books, call toll free 1-800-542-2595 or fax 1-877-542-2596.

Library of Congress Cataloging-in-Publication Data

Names: Saxena, Shalini, 1982- author.
Title: Nero : ruthless Roman Emperor / Shalini Saxena.
Description: New York : Gareth Stevens Publishing, [2017] | Series: History's
    most murderous villains | Includes index.
Identifiers: LCCN 2016008670 | ISBN 9781482447996 (pbk.) | ISBN 9781482448016
    (library bound) | ISBN 9781482448009 (6 pack)
Subjects: LCSH: Nero, Emperor of Rome, 37-68-Juvenile literature. |
    Emperors-Rome-Biography-Juvenile literature. | Rome-History-Nero,
    54-68-Juvenile literature.
Classification: LCC DG285 .S28 2016 | DDC 937/.07092-dc23
LC record available at http://lccn.loc.gov/2016008670

First Edition

Published in 2017 by
Gareth Stevens Publishing
111 East 14th Street, Suite 349
New York, NY 10003

Designer: Katelyn E. Reynolds
Editor: Therese Shea

Photo credits: Cover, p. 1 (Nero) Ann Ronan Pictures/Print Collector/Getty Images;
cover, pp. 1-32 (background texture) Eky Studio/Shutterstock.com; cover, pp. 1-32
(blood background) Kjpargeter/Shutterstock.com; cover, pp. 1-32 (grunge banner)
Miloje/Shutterstock.com; p. 5 Florilegius/SSPL/GettyImages; pp. 7, 16-17, 29 Hulton
Archive/Getty Images; p. 9 (map) ColdEel/Wikipedia.org; p. 9 (inset) DEA/A. DAGLI
ORTI/De Agostini Picture Library/Getty Images; p. 11 Kean Collection/Getty Images;
pp. 12, 19 Werner Forman/Universal Images Group/Getty Images; p. 15 De Agostini
Picture Library/Getty Images; p. 21 New York Public Library/Science Source/Getty
Images; p. 22 DEA/P. DE ANTONIS/De Agostini/Getty Images; p. 23 ALBERTO
PIZZOLI/AFP/Getty Images; ; p. 25 DEA PICTURE LIBRARY/Getty Images; p. 27
SuperStock/Getty Images.

Printed in the United States of America

CPSIA compliance information: Batch #CS16GS: For further information contact Gareth Stevens, New York, New York at 1-800-542-2595.

CONTENTS

WORDS IN THE GLOSSARY APPEAR IN BOLD TYPE
THE FIRST TIME THEY ARE USED IN THE TEXT.

A PUBLIC SPECTACLE

The crowd gazed uncomfortably at the stage, listening to the singer's almost comically weak voice. They sat clapping, just as they had been told to do. They had been clapping for hours—even though an earthquake had struck moments earlier. Normally, many would have left already, but this performance was different. Commoners and soldiers had gathered in this theater to listen to a very important singer: the Roman emperor Nero.

It was unheard of for a leader to take part in public entertainment, but Nero loved the sound of clapping. He didn't allow anyone to leave a performance for any reason—not even an earthquake. In *De Vita Caesarum* (*Lives of the Caesars*), Roman historian Suetonius wrote, "It is said that some women gave birth to children there." Such was Nero's tyranny.

TERRIBLE TRUTHS

The word "emperor" comes from the Latin word *imperator*, a title given to a general who was victorious in war. After the Roman Empire was founded, it came to mean "ruler."

THE ROMAN EMPIRE

THE ROMAN EMPIRE LASTED FROM 27 BC UNTIL AD 476. BEFORE THEN, ROME WAS A REPUBLIC RUN BY WEALTHY CITIZENS. ROME IS IN PRESENT-DAY ITALY, BUT AT ITS HEIGHT, THE ROMAN EMPIRE INCLUDED MANY PARTS OF WESTERN EUROPE, THE MIDDLE EAST, AND NORTHERN AFRICA. ROMAN EMPERORS RULED OVER THE ENTIRE EMPIRE. SOME EMPERORS WERE BELOVED BY THEIR CITIZENS, WHILE OTHERS, LIKE NERO, MISUSED THEIR POWER AND WERE WIDELY HATED. ROMAN EMPERORS TOOK THE TITLE "CAESAR."

‹ NERO

Nero believed he could excel at anything. He learned how to play different musical instruments, sing, act, and drive a **chariot**.

A TROUBLED FAMILY TREE

Nero was born Lucius Domitius Ahenobarbus in 37 BC. Viciousness and a hunger for power ran deep in his blood. Suetonius describes Nero's father, Gnaeus Domitius Ahenobarbus, as "hateful in every walk of life." He once ran over a boy with his chariot for no reason. Gnaeus died when Nero was 2 or 3, so he was raised by his mother, Agrippina the Younger.

Agrippina's brother was the mad emperor Caligula. After Caligula was murdered for his cruelty, her uncle Claudius became emperor. Desperate for Nero to become ruler one day, Agrippina helped plot the murder of Claudius's wife. She then married her uncle, who adopted Nero. Agrippina's plotting worked. She convinced Claudius to name Nero the next emperor over his own son.

TERRIBLE TRUTHS

In addition to marrying her uncle after having his wife killed, Agrippina the Younger poisoned her previous husband, had her opponents in Claudius's court killed, and most likely poisoned Claudius, too.

THE MAD EMPEROR CALIGULA

Nero's uncle Caligula is remembered for his madness and his **brutality**, which may have been the result of a serious illness. He did many strange and evil things. For example, he made senators run in front of his chariot for long distances, just to make them suffer. Caligula once called off a battle and ordered his soldiers to fill their helmets with seashells. He would kill anyone who mentioned goats in front of him.

Agrippina the Younger, like many members of her family, was often plotting evil schemes.

A PROMISING START

Claudius died in the year AD 54, after eating a bowl of (probably poisoned) mushrooms. Nero, who wasn't even 17, was then made emperor. The young emperor's reign began well enough. His close advisors were Sextus Afranius Burrus, a member of the **Praetorian Guard**, and Lucius Annaeus Seneca, a philosopher and Nero's old tutor.

With the guidance of Burrus and Seneca, Nero ended many of the brutal practices of earlier emperors. He allowed slaves to make complaints against masters who treated them unfairly. He didn't punish those who complained about him or plotted against him.

Nero also introduced competitions in poetry and athletics and promoted the arts and theater. Taxes were lowered, cities that suffered misfortunes received help, and death sentences ended. Overall, Romans were content.

TERRIBLE TRUTHS

In ancient Rome, citizens could be sentenced to death in different ways for a wide range of crimes. Some were killed by animals while the public watched, others were burned alive, and still others were crucified, or nailed to a cross.

SENECA THE YOUNGER

Nero's advisor Seneca, or Seneca the Younger, was more than a tutor and advisor. He was a famous ancient Roman philosopher, often writing about his views on what is right and wrong. He also covered other subjects. Additionally, Seneca wrote many plays that influenced later playwrights, including William Shakespeare. In one of his works, called *De Ira* (*On Anger*), Seneca says the following about governing: "No one can rule who cannot also submit to authority."

THE ROMAN EMPIRE IN AD 54

London

Gaul

Aquileia

Marseilles

Italy

Rome

Illyricum

Macedonia

Spain

Bithynia and Pontus

Pisidia

Cappadocia

Achaia

Pamphylia

Cilicia

Cordoba

Greece

Lycia

Antioch

Cypres

Syria

Crete

Carthage

Jerusalem

Alexandria

Africa

Egypt

Although Nero was the emperor, many believed Seneca, seen here, and Burrus were the real rulers in Nero's early years. Nero's peaceful first 5 years as emperor were called the *quinquennium Neronis*.

L. ANNÆVS SENECA.

A MURDEROUS STREAK

Agrippina had long tried to control Nero, but both Seneca and Burrus felt that Nero would be better off ruling without her. They forced her to retire in AD 56. The less power Agrippina had, the more she turned against her son.

Agrippina began to encourage Nero's stepbrother Britannicus to act against Nero and become ruler. Nero found out about her plans, and he poisoned Britannicus.

Nero then turned his attention to his mother. He first tried to sink a boat in which Agrippina was sailing. The boat sank, but Agrippina survived. In his work *Annals*, Roman historian Tacitus reported that Agrippina said: "I believe nothing about my son; he has not ordered his mother's murder." Unfortunately for her, Nero tried again and succeeded. In AD 59, he had Agrippina stabbed to death.

TERRIBLE TRUTHS

It was also rumored that Nero tried to kill his mother by making the ceiling over her bed collapse. That, too, didn't work.

Roman Historians

Much of what we know about Nero is thanks to the written observations of historians such as Tacitus and Suetonius. Tacitus was an ORATOR and public official. He discusses Nero, Agrippina, and more in his work *Annales* (*Annals*). Suetonius's most famous work is *De Vita Caesarum* (*Lives of the Caesars*), which covers the lives and reigns of Rome's first 12 emperors. Suetonius once studied law, too. Knowing about many subjects allowed these historians to make intelligent observations about their society and rulers.

Nero told the Senate that he had to kill Agrippina because she was planning to kill him. The senators believed him, and he wasn't punished for the crime. The dead woman is pictured here.

11

Despite being friends with Poppaea's husband, Otho, Nero had him sent away so he could marry Poppaea, seen here.

With his mother out of the way and with Seneca and Burrus doing much of the ruling of the empire, Nero was free to do whatever he wanted. Nero had married Claudius's daughter Octavia before becoming emperor, but he didn't love her. He fell in love with Poppaea Sabina, the wife of a senator who was also his friend.

Nero feared Octavia would turn the public against him after finding out about his affection for Poppaea, so he divorced her. However, Nero worried that if she lived, the public would question if he should remain emperor without her. After all, she was the daughter of Claudius, and he was only a stepson. In AD 62, Nero had Octavia killed, and he married Poppaea.

TERRIBLE TRUTHS

Nero had tried several times to choke Octavia to death before divorcing her. He then had her killed.

PERSONAL PLEASURES

As much death as there was around him, Nero's life wasn't all about killing. In fact, he seemed to prefer using his time to learn and create. He supported the arts both in public and in private. Nero dined with poets, tried his hand at a stringed instrument called the lyre, and loved to sing.

These interests might seem harmless, but the public expected emperors to put the empire's interests above their own. Still, Nero did as he pleased. He acted in plays. He went so far as to put on public performances of his singing and lyre playing.

Nero isn't remembered as being particularly talented. Bad or good, audiences were forced to sit through every performance—some of which lasted hours—and could never speak against him.

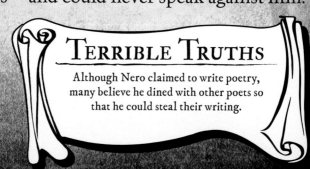

TERRIBLE TRUTHS

Although Nero claimed to write poetry, many believe he dined with other poets so that he could steal their writing.

POETRY IN ANCIENT ROME

Along with music and drama, poetry was a form of entertainment in Roman life. People would gather to hear others read their poems. By the time of the Roman Empire, poems could be about almost anything, including love, history, and society in general. Virgil is perhaps Rome's most famous poet. He wrote the *Aeneid*, which is about Rome's founding. In it he writes, "Young Romulus will take the leadership . . . And call by his own name his people Romans."

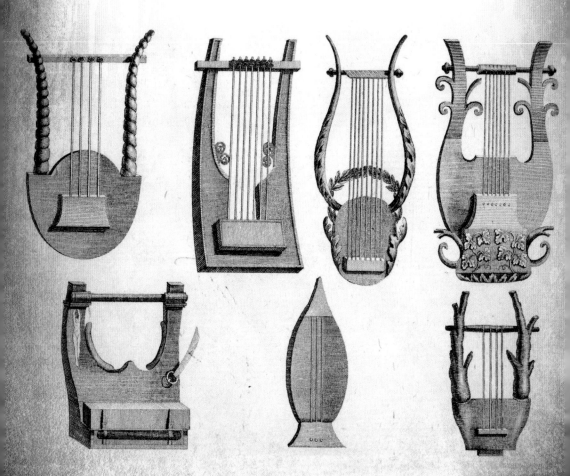

Ancient Romans and Greeks used different kinds of lyres to play different kinds of songs. Lyres were often played before someone read poetry.

Chariot racing drew huge crowds to the Circus Maximus.

The arts weren't Nero's only passion. He also enjoyed athletic activities such as chariot racing, which was popular among Rome's public. Emperors and other members of the upper classes usually didn't participate in such events. Nero didn't care. Tacitus commented that crowds were "delighted if the emperor shares their tastes."

Nero loved horses and even raced himself. Most chariots were drawn by two, four, or six horses. Nero entered the Olympic Games of AD 67 with a 10-horse chariot. In the middle of the games, the horses threw Nero from his chariot. He never finished the race. Yet somehow, he still won! That's because Nero had bribed the judges with enormous amounts of money to give him first place.

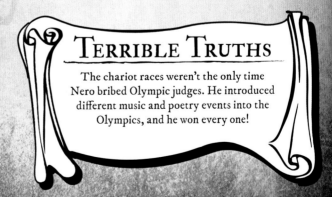

TERRIBLE TRUTHS

The chariot races weren't the only time Nero bribed Olympic judges. He introduced different music and poetry events into the Olympics, and he won every one!

A TURNING POINT

Despite Nero's strange and dangerous actions, daily life in Rome was generally normal until AD 62. In that year, Burrus died, and Nero replaced him with two new advisors, Faenius Rufus and Gaius Ofonius Tigellinus. Tigellinus only encouraged Nero's bad behavior and went so far as to reintroduce unpopular practices that Seneca and Burrus had ended.

Seneca refused to tolerate these changes and retired soon after. With no one to discourage him, Nero got worse. He continued to perform in public, threw wild parties, and had Roman citizens killed for speaking out against him or for no reason at all.

By this time, there was unrest in Roman territories, too. Nero had been using money from these areas on buildings, gifts, and **extravagances**. People began to revolt.

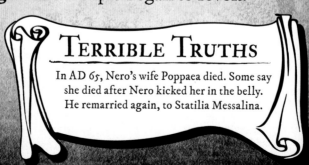

TERRIBLE TRUTHS

In AD 65, Nero's wife Poppaea died. Some say she died after Nero kicked her in the belly. He remarried again, to Statilia Messalina.

TIGELLINUS

GAIUS OFONIUS TIGELLINUS WAS IN MANY WAYS JUST AS CRUEL AS NERO. TIGELLINUS HAD LIVED IN CALIGULA'S HOUSEHOLD. TACITUS WROTE THAT HE HAD A "VICIOUS CHILDHOOD." HE WAS THE HEAD OF ROME'S FIRE BRIGADE BEFORE BECOMING HEAD OF THE PRAETORIAN GUARD. HE ENCOURAGED NERO TO TAKE REVENGE ON HIS ENEMIES AND MAY HAVE HAD A HAND IN OCTAVIA'S DEATH. WHEN POPPAEA'S FIRST HUSBAND, OTHO, LATER BECAME EMPEROR, OTHO ORDERED TIGELLINUS TO KILL HIMSELF.

This coin shows Nero with either Tigellinus or Rufus addressing the Praetorian Guard. Nero hoped such an image would make him seem like a military leader.

THE GREAT FIRE
OF ROME

On July 19, AD 64, a fire began near the Circus Maximus. The flames spread quickly, tearing through the city for 9 days, destroying two-thirds of it before dying down. By then, Nero had made it known that he wanted to tear down parts of Rome to make room for newer, more magnificent buildings. So when the fire started, many understandably believed Nero was responsible. However, Nero had already left Rome for his summer home in Antium, which was 35 miles (56 km) away.

Although Nero didn't start the fire himself, many still felt he did little to help. Tacitus famously wrote, "A rumor had spread that, while the city was burning, Nero . . . had sung of the destruction of Troy." Eager to find someone else to blame, Nero pointed to a small religious group: Christians.

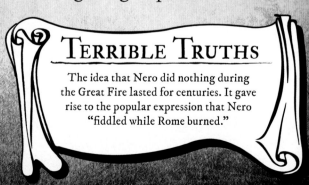

TERRIBLE TRUTHS

The idea that Nero did nothing during the Great Fire lasted for centuries. It gave rise to the popular expression that Nero "fiddled while Rome burned."

RELIGION IN ROME

At the time of Nero's reign, most Romans worshipped the gods of Roman myth, such as Jupiter, Juno, and Pluto, who were believed to control different aspects of life on Earth. There were few Christians and Jews in the Roman Empire then. According to both religions, there's only one god. Many people, including Nero, felt that Christians and Jews couldn't be trusted because they didn't worship Roman gods. Both groups often clashed with Romans in different parts of the Empire.

Despite popular ideas, Nero couldn't have "fiddled" while Rome burned, as the fiddle hadn't been invented yet. He might have sung about Troy, as Tacitus wrote. Troy was a famous city written about in ancient stories and poems.

At the time of the Great Fire, Christianity was still a minor religion in the Roman Empire. Many thought Christian beliefs were strange and evil. For this reason, Nero thought that he could blame the fire on Christians, even though they were innocent. Christians were **persecuted** in Rome as a result. Many were killed. Some were burned alive, while others were torn to pieces by animals as Romans looked on.

Having found others to blame for the fire, Nero turned to different matters. He used the fire as an excuse to move forward with his plan to rebuild the city as he saw fit. He admired the buildings of ancient Greece and had parts of the city built in Greek style. One product of this appreciation was the Domus Aurea, or "Golden House."

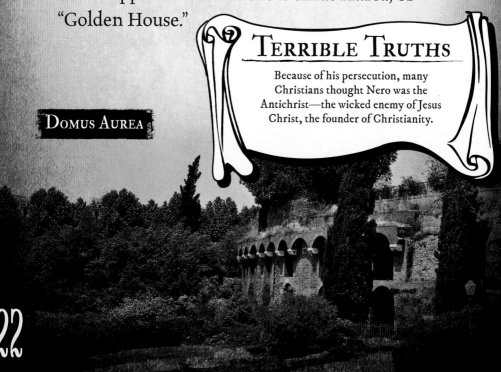

DOMUS AUREA

TERRIBLE TRUTHS

Because of his persecution, many Christians thought Nero was the Antichrist—the wicked enemy of Jesus Christ, the founder of Christianity.

THE GOLDEN HOUSE OF NERO

THE GOLDEN HOUSE WAS AN ENORMOUS AND ELABORATE PALACE AND PARK THAT SPANNED OVER 200 ACRES (81 HA), LINKING SEVERAL HILLS IN ROME. THE BUILDING HAD HUNDREDS OF ROOMS, LINED WITH GOLD AND PRECIOUS STONES. THE SURROUNDING PARK HAD BEAUTIFUL FOUNTAINS, BATHS, AND SCULPTURES. THERE WAS EVEN A MAN-MADE LAKE AND A MASSIVE BRONZE STATUE OF NERO HIMSELF. ACCORDING TO SUETONIUS, NERO REMARKED THAT THE GOLDEN HOUSE MEANT HE COULD FINALLY "BEGIN TO LIVE LIKE A HUMAN BEING."

Archaeologists and historians are working today to protect the remains of the Golden House. Although it was beautiful, many Romans felt it was another example of Nero working for his own pleasure rather than theirs.

A FAILED PLOT

After the fire and his wasteful building in Rome, Nero started to become very unpopular. He even lost the support of the Senate, which had tolerated him until then. Something had to be done. In AD 65, 41 military officials, senators, philosophers, and others came together over their distrust of Nero. They hatched a plot to have Nero killed so they could make Gaius Calpurnius Piso, a popular orator, the new emperor. This plot became known as the Pisonian **Conspiracy**.

The plan might have succeeded. However, Nero's slaves found out about the conspiracy and warned their master. Nero reacted quickly. Eighteen of the people involved, including Piso, were either killed or ordered to kill themselves. Others were sent away. Some were even cleared and forgiven.

TERRIBLE TRUTHS

One of the people who died after Nero discovered the conspiracy was Seneca. Nero ordered that Seneca kill himself, so he drank poison.

SLAVERY IN ROME

SLAVES WERE THE LOWEST CLASS OF ROMAN SOCIETY. THEY
WERE CONSIDERED PROPERTY, NOT PEOPLE. SLAVES BELONGED
TO THEIR OWNERS AND WORKED EVERYWHERE FROM HOMES
TO PUBLIC PLACES. OWNERS COULD FREE SLAVES, BUT MANY
TREATED THEM BADLY. SOME PEOPLE WERE BORN SLAVES,
BUT OTHERS BECAME SLAVES AFTER BEING CONQUERED OR
CAPTURED IN WAR. SENECA BELIEVED SLAVES SHOULD BE
TREATED BETTER. HE WROTE IN HIS *MORAL EPISTLES*: "WE
MALTREAT THEM . . . AS IF THEY WERE BEASTS OF BURDEN."

When he heard his death sentence, Seneca didn't resist.
He accepted his fate and killed himself as ordered.

CHAOS IN THE EMPIRE

Rome wasn't the only place in the empire facing problems. By AD 66, many provinces of the Roman Empire had started to revolt. In Armenia, for example, a new king had come to power because Armenians disliked Roman rule. Nero's army allowed the king to remain, but forced him to serve Nero. In Judaea, the First Jewish Revolt began in AD 66 and didn't end until AD 70.

To make matters worse, around this time, Nero took a 15-month-long vacation to Greece. There he walked around in strange clothing with no shoes and long hair. He freed some Greek cities of Roman rule. He also continued to act in public, playing roles thought highly unsuitable for an emperor. Romans had had enough.

TERRIBLE TRUTHS

Gaius Julius Vindex, a **legate** who would lead a revolt against Nero, said of him, "I have seen him on stage playing pregnant women and slaves about to be executed."

THE FIRST JEWISH REVOLT

Judaea, in what is now Israel, first came under Roman rule in 63 BC. The Jewish people who lived there came into conflict with Roman officials over taxes and other issues. In AD 66, a Roman official stole silver from the Temple, a sacred site. Jews came together to revolt. Nero sent in his own forces to retake Judaea for Rome. The Temple was destroyed, and the Roman army crushed the Jewish fighters in AD 70. More than 40,000 Jews were killed.

Nero sent future emperor Vespasian to end the Jewish revolt. He was joined by his son Titus, another future emperor. Their forces destroyed the city and the Jewish Temple.

THE REIGN OF TERROR ENDS

Nero didn't return from Greece until February of AD 68. Revolting continued in Spain and Gaul (now France), which Nero did nothing to stop. The revolt in Spain ended when the governor, Servius Sulpicius Galba, was made emperor. Seeing Galba as a true leader, the Senate threw their support to him. Nero was named a "public enemy" and sentenced to death by whipping on a cross—the way slaves were sentenced to die at the time.

Though Nero wanted to escape, he realized he was out of time and decided to kill himself instead. Nero stabbed himself in the throat on June 9 in AD 68 and quickly died. Suetonius reported the emperor's last **laments**. Among them was: "What an artist the world is losing!"

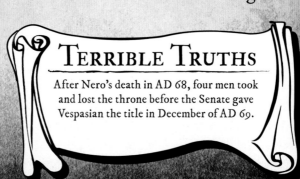

TERRIBLE TRUTHS

After Nero's death in AD 68, four men took and lost the throne before the Senate gave Vespasian the title in December of AD 69.

Remembering Nero

It may be easy to think that Nero's death was a good thing for Rome and the empire. However, historians now remember Nero with mixed reactions. Nero supported arts and building projects, which became an important part of Roman culture. We still admire many of those today. Nero also rebuilt Rome after the fire. Yet Nero was most definitely a brutal tyrant, too. Romans wouldn't soon forget his cruelty, persecutions, and the overall misery he caused.

Nero's death meant the end of the Julio-Claudian **dynasty**, the four rulers after Augustus, the first Roman emperor: Tiberius (reigned AD 14–37), Caligula (AD 37–41), Claudius I (AD 41–54), and Nero (AD 54–68).

29

GLOSSARY

brigade: a group of people organized to act

brutality: cruel or violent treatment of others

chariot: a carriage with two wheels that was pulled by horses and was raced and used in battle in ancient times

conspiracy: a secret plan made by two or more people to do something that is harmful or illegal

dynasty: a family of rulers

extravagance: a special purchase that costs more than is usual

lament: an expression of sorrow or unhappiness

legate: an official representative sent to a foreign government

orator: someone skilled in public speaking

persecute: to treat in a cruel or violent way because of differences in belief or behavior

Praetorian Guard: soldiers that protected the Roman emperor

republic: a government run by elected representatives

FOR MORE INFORMATION

BOOKS

Crompton, Samuel Willard. *Discovering Ancient Rome.* New York, NY: Britannica Educational Publishing, 2015.

Williams, Marcia. *The Romans: Gods, Emperors, and Dormice.* Somerville, MA: Candlewick Press, 2013.

Zumbusch, Amelie von. *Ancient Roman Government.* New York, NY: PowerKids Press, 2014.

WEBSITES

Nero: Fun Facts and Information
www.funtrivia.com/en/History/Nero-17771.html
Test your knowledge about Nero on this site, which features trivia questions.

Nero Timeline
www.ancient.eu/timeline/Nero/
This site summarizes the major events of Nero's life in a timeline.

INDEX